D0382099

Adolf Hitler

Katie Daynes

Designed by Karen Tomlins

History consultant: Prof. Dr. Joachim Fest

Reading consultant: Alison Kelly, Roehampton University

WITHDRAWN

CONTRA COSTA COUNTY LIBRARY

3 1901 04269 4002

Edited by Jane Chisholm   Cover design by Russell Punter
Digital imaging by Keith Furnival

First published in 2006 by Usborne Publishing Ltd., Usborne House,
83-85 Saffron Hill, London EC1N 8RT, England. www.usborne.com
Copyright © 2006 Usborne Publishing Ltd. The name Usborne and the
devices 🜨 are Trade Marks of Usborne Publishing Ltd.

All rights reserved. No part of this publication may be reproduced,
stored in a retrieval system or transmitted in any form or by any means,
electronic, mechanical, photocopying, recording or otherwise,
without the prior permission of the publisher. Printed in China. UE.
First published in America in 2006.

ACKNOWLEDGEMENTS

© akg-images p35; © Bavarian State Library, Munich p47 (Heinrich Hoffmann);
© Bridgeman Art Library p25 (Held Collection), © CORBIS front cover (Hulton-Deutsch
Collection), back cover (Michael Nicholson), p1 (Bettmann), pp2-3 (Bettmann), p7, pp10-11,
p12 (Bettmann), p13 (Harald A. Jahn), p16 (Stephanie Colasanti), p19 (Austrian Archives),
p21 (Austrian Archives), pp22-23 (Hulton-Deutsch Collection), p26 (Sean Sexton Collection),
p27 (Bettmann), p31 (Hulton-Deutsch Collection), pp32-33 (Hulton-Deutsch Collection), pp40-41,
p44 (Bettmann), p49 left (Michael Nicholson), p53 (Bettmann), p57, pp58-59, (Bettmann), p59
top (Museum of Flight), p60; © Getty images p34 (Hulton Archive), pp54-55 (Hulton Archive),
p63 (Hulton Archive); © MARY EVANS PICTURE LIBRARY pp28-29, p37 (Weimar Archive),
p39, pp42-43, p45, p49 right, pp50-51, p56, p58; © popperfoto.com p5, p6, p9;
© TopFoto.co.uk pp14-15
Every effort has been made to trace and acknowledge ownership of copyright.
The publishers offer to rectify any omissions in future editions, following notification.

Adolf Hitler salutes the Parade
of Flags at Nuremberg, 1935.

Contents

A map of Europe in 1933, when Hitler came to power

Internet links

You can find out more about Adolf Hitler and the Second World War by going to the Usborne Quicklinks Website at **www.usborne-quicklinks.com** and typing in the keyword **Hitler**.

At the Usborne Quicklinks Website you will find direct links to a selection of recommended websites. Here are a few of the things you can do:

- Listen to Hitler making a speech.
- See film footage of the German invasion of Poland.
- Take a virtual tour of a Nazi concentration camp.

The recommended websites are regularly reviewed and updated but please note, Usborne Publishing is not responsible for the content of any website other than its own.

Adolf Hitler
as a baby

Chapter 1

A reluctant student

The woods outside the Austrian town of
Linz rustled with boys playing war games.

"Bags be the leader of the Boer army,"
cried a thin, pale boy named Adolf Hitler.
"You can be the English. Give us five minutes
to hide, then come and get us!"

Adolf loved organizing battles after
school – so long as he won. When he
wasn't outside plotting ambushes, he liked
to lose himself in a fantasy world of cowboys
and Indians.

"Bang-bang, bang," he cried, firing an imaginary pistol at his baby sister, Paula. Then a door slammed shut, making the whole house shudder. "Dad's back," gasped Adolf. He ran to his room to avoid his father's temper. Curled up in bed, Adolf read another daring tale of adventure and gunfights in the Wild West.

Adolf started secondary school, aged 11. It was his father's idea to send him to a *Realschule*, where they taught mainly science and technical skills. But Adolf was a reluctant student. He much preferred drawing and writing to science and numbers. And he resented the hour-long walk to and from the school.

Adolf in a school photo, aged 8

By the end of the first year, he had done very little work and received 'unsatisfactory' grades for two of his subjects. The teachers said he must repeat the year.

"What?" cried Adolf's father, when he heard the news. "At this rate, you'll never be able to get a government job."

Adolf stared sullenly through steely blue eyes. His father had been a civil servant for 40 years and he expected Adolf to do the same. But Adolf had other ideas. "I don't need to study," he said, firmly. "I'm going to be an artist."

Adolf's father,
Alois Hitler

His father's face turned scarlet with rage. "An artist, no!" he cried. "Never – as long as I live!"

Adolf returned to school with gritted teeth, and continued to spend more time doodling than taking notes.

7

A year later, his father was drinking his usual morning glass of wine, when he suddenly collapsed and died. Adolf didn't feel sad. He felt liberated. Now he was master of his own destiny.

"Remember your father's wishes..." pleaded his mother.

"Don't worry, Mother," he replied. "I know what's best for me."

He had no intention of working for the government, but he didn't know how to become an artist. After failing more exams, he was transferred to another school, even further from home. It was too far to travel each day, so he had to find a place to stay in the local town.

Adolf didn't care for his latest school, or its staff, and he didn't bother making friends with other students. The only subjects that interested him were drawing and physical education. Each evening he spent alone in a shabby little room.

Two years later, at the age of 16, Adolf finished school and moved back to Linz. He still had no plan, but a couple of idle years at home suited him perfectly. He spent the days drawing, painting, reading and writing, while his mother, sister and Aunt Johanna cooked and cleaned for him.

Adolf, aged 16, sketched by a fellow student

Adolf wasn't interested in a social life, but he did love going to the opera, especially operas by the German composer Richard Wagner. One evening he met another teenager who shared his passion – August Kubizek, or Gustl for short.

"No one writes music like Wagner," declared Adolf, with great enthusiasm.

"I know," agreed Gustl, eagerly. "His tunes are so powerful."

9

"And heroic," Adolf added. They had just watched *Lohengrin*, the story of a knight who rescues a maiden, only to be betrayed by her. Throughout Adolf's life it remained the opera he loved most.

Soon, Adolf and Gustl were meeting up most evenings. They wandered the streets of Linz deep in conversation. Usually Adolf lectured while Gustl listened. His latest topic was architecture.

"These buildings are an eyesore!" Adolf ranted. "We should pull them down and build something grander."

During the day, Gustl earned a living in his father's workshop, but Adolf never earned a penny. He lazed at home, daydreaming and sketching his own designs for Linz's buildings.

That spring, Adolf decided to see some real architecture. He talked his mother into funding a trip to Austria's capital city, Vienna. He journeyed alone and spent two weeks wandering the streets as a tourist. Adolf was enchanted.

This is how Vienna looked when Adolf Hitler first visited in 1906. The majestic buildings and open spaces were unlike anything he'd seen before.

He went back to Linz with a clearer vision for his future. He would move to Vienna and excel as a student at the Academy of Fine Arts. No advice from his relatives about finding a serious career could persuade him otherwise.

But then he received the devastating news that his mother had breast cancer.

"I'm afraid she's unlikely to survive," announced the family doctor, a Jew named Dr. Bloch.

Adolf felt his eyes prickle with tears. His father had been a bossy brute, but his mother was always so kind and tender. How could fate take away the one person he loved?

Adolf's mother, Klara Hitler

As spring turned to summer, Adolf stayed at home and watched, helpless, as his mother's health deteriorated.

One afternoon he took her hand in his. "The entrance exams for the Art Academy are in September," he told her quietly.

"Then you must go," she said. "You must think of your future."

This photograph shows one of the grand halls in the Academy of Fine Arts, Vienna, where Adolf Hitler wanted to study.

The next day, armed with bundles of drawings, Adolf set off for Vienna. Based on the strength of his work, the Academy allowed him to take the two entrance exams.

For three hours at a time, Adolf sat sketching with confidence. At the age of 18, he felt he was pursuing his dream.

Hitler did this drawing of the
Ringstrasse in Vienna in 1914.

The last thing he expected was rejection.

"Test drawing unsatisfactory," stated the examiner's report. "Not enough heads."

"There must be some mistake," cried Adolf. "I am a great artist!" He tracked down the Rector of the Academy and demanded an explanation.

"We feel your talent lies in line drawing, not painting," answered the Rector. "Have you thought of becoming an architect?"

It took several days for Adolf to calm down. By then, his mother was gravely ill, so he rushed back to be by her side. He doted on her, as she had doted on him, but he was powerless to save her. Four days before Christmas, she died peacefully. And Adolf's future was less certain than ever.

Chapter 2

The drop-out

In February, Adolf returned to Vienna. With a small inheritance from his mother and a monthly orphan's pension, he had just enough money to live on. He rented a small room from a Polish woman and begged his friend Gustl to join him.

"All of Vienna is waiting for you," he promised on a postcard. "Beg you again, come soon!"

And Gustl did. He was lured by Adolf's descriptions of the city... and the possibility of studying music at the Vienna Conservatoire.

When Gustl arrived it was already evening and he was exhausted after his long journey. But Adolf wouldn't let him rest.

"There's a whole city to see!" he cried. "You can't sleep until I've at least shown you the Court Opera House."

Adolf and Gustl had little money between them, so they decided to share a room. It was very cramped for two, especially when Gustl rented a grand piano.

Adolf Hitler and his friend Gustl spent many evenings at the Court Opera House in Vienna, pictured below.

Gustl was a truly gifted pianist and he was quickly awarded a place at the Conservatoire. "Now we can both study during the day and go to operas in the evening," said Gustl, delighted.

Adolf forced a thin smile. He had been too proud to tell anyone that he had failed the Academy entrance exam. While Gustl left every morning for the Conservatoire, Adolf lounged in bed, went for walks, leafed through books and sketched furiously. When they were both in the room, there was hardly space to breathe.

"If you play that scale one more time..." fumed Adolf, jumping to his feet. "What are they teaching you anyway? They're no better than the Art Academy."

Gustl was shocked. "What do you mean?" he asked.

"They rejected me," Adolf blurted out. "They threw me out, turned me down."

"Oh Adolf," sighed Gustl. "Why didn't

you say! What are you going to do now?"

That question made Adolf lose his temper completely. The truth was, he had no idea.

Over the following months, he busied himself formulating grand plans. One week, he started to write an opera, the next he decided to sketch improvements for Vienna's residential buildings. The rest of the time he spent drawing, or reading avidly from his new library book, *Legends of Gods and Heroes*. He spent very little money on food or drink. In fact, his only extravagance was going to the opera.

That summer, Gustl went home to visit his parents. Alone in Vienna, Adolf still had his mind fixed on becoming a great artist. So he applied to the Art Academy again.

"They can't reject me twice," he reasoned. But he was wrong. This time, they didn't even allow him to take the exams. Stunned and defeated, Adolf descended into a bitter depression.

Rather than admit his failure to Gustl, he moved out of their room, leaving no explanation. He rented a large, airy room that he could barely afford. On the busy street below, there was a kiosk selling cheap, trashy magazines. To while away the hours, Adolf devoured one magazine after another – and was fascinated by what he read.

This illustration promotes one of the many newspapers on sale when Hitler was in Vienna.

According to the magazine *Ostara*, blonde, blue-eyed Germans were natural rulers. They were a heroic master race who could lead the nation to success and greatness. Meanwhile, there was an underclass of dark 'beast-men' who were responsible for all the ills in the world. "Blonde people unite!" proclaimed the magazine. "Together we can build a better future."

Adolf found the idea of a master race very appealing. He wasn't blonde, but he did have blue eyes and he spoke German. Suddenly he was aware of the thousands of foreigners scurrying about the streets. It was reassuring to think that *they* were to blame for his own misfortune.

By now, he had spent his inheritance from his mother. Still too proud to find a job, he only had his orphan's pension to live on, and that didn't even cover the rent.

A year after leaving Gustl, 20-year-old Adolf was forced to join the beggars and drunks of Vienna, living rough on the streets and rummaging through bins for scraps to eat. He slept in the open while the good weather lasted, but then the Austrian winter set in.

Shivering in the last glimmer of daylight, Adolf pulled up the collar of his shabby blue suit. Two beggars were talking beside him.

"Let's try out that new hostel near the Schönbrunn Palace," said one. "I'm dying for a good night's sleep."

Adolf followed the men at a distance. That night, he had his first bath in months. His clothes were disinfected and there was soup and bread for supper.

Hitler lived rough on the streets, like these Viennese beggars, photographed in 1900.

Lying awake on his dormitory bed, Adolf could have felt grateful, but he just felt disgusted. "I am not like these people," he told himself. "I belong to a master race. I shouldn't even be here."

The next evening, a young man struck up a conversation with him. "You look miserable," he said. "Have some bread."

Adolf grunted and took a chunk.

"Call me Fritz," he added cheerfully. "I'm from Germany."

As Fritz described his life in Germany's capital, Berlin, Adolf found himself listening eagerly. Vienna may have let him down, but there were still far greater cities to visit.

More immediately, Adolf needed money. Fritz took him to shovel snow for cash. With no coat, Adolf didn't last long in the cold, so he offered to carry people's bags at the station instead. But no one trusted him with their belongings.

In the dormitory that evening, Fritz was exasperated. "What *can* you do?" he asked.

"I am a great artist," said Adolf, with less conviction than usual. Deep down, he was afraid of being a nobody.

Adolf was close to despair when a letter arrived from his Aunt Johanna. Concerned about her wayward nephew, she had enclosed a generous sum of money.

"I can buy myself a coat!" cried Adolf.

"We can go into business!" cried Fritz. The plan was for Adolf to paint views of Vienna, and for Fritz to sell them in local beer halls.

Hitler briefly tried to earn money by clearing snow off the streets, like the men pictured below.

As their business idea began to make them money, they moved to a more comfortable hostel – the Men's Home. Adolf chose to paint in the public writing room, where a select group of residents gathered each day. They called themselves the 'intellectuals' and they enjoyed animated discussions about politics and art.

Adolf was soon adding his own strong opinions. "The Austrian state is to blame for letting foreigners run riot," he ranted.

To Fritz's frustration, Adolf spent more time debating than painting. "We could be making much more money," he sighed.

"But you still haven't paid me for the last two paintings," replied Adolf, brusquely.

When Fritz denied the accusation, Adolf reported him to the police and asked a Jew to sell his paintings instead. He stayed at the Men's Home for two more years. The others saw him as an eccentric artist, with strong anti-government beliefs. He seldom strayed

This is one of Hitler's paintings, showing market stalls in a Viennese square.

from the oak table by the window and sold just enough paintings to pay his keep.

In fact, Adolf was only passing time. For on his 24th birthday he would receive his father's inheritance.

"I'm going to study art in Germany," he told the residents. As soon as the money came through, he packed his few belongings into a black suitcase and left for the nearest German city, Munich.

25

Chapter 3

The joy of war

When Adolf saw Munich it was love at first sight. The wide boulevards, the art galleries, the imposing architecture – everything oozed Germanic power and greatness.

Hitler was instantly impressed by the grand buildings in Munich. This vast gateway marks the entrance to one of Munich's main squares.

Hitler sold his paintings in Munich beer halls
like this one, photographed in 1913.

But Adolf's life was far from grand. He
decided against art school. "What can
others teach me that I don't already know?"
he reasoned. Instead, he continued
painting postcard-sized street scenes and
sold them in local beer halls.

While Adolf had no close friends to
speak of, he enjoyed the chatter in beer
halls and cafés. Cheap newspapers kept
him up-to-date with current events and beer
drinkers made a perfect audience for his
political rants.

A year later, the streets of Munich were alive with gossip.

"The Austrian Archduke has been assassinated," was the news on everyone's lips. "Serbia is to blame."

Adolf felt a prickle of excitement and rushed to his nearest beer hall. The regulars were involved in a heated debate...

"The Austrians will want revenge."

"They're going to attack Serbia."

"But then the Russians will retaliate."

"Good!" chipped in Adolf. "If Russia threatens Austria, Germany will have the perfect excuse to fight a glorious war."

Adolf wasn't alone in his enthusiasm. Many Germans wanted to fight for greater power and influence in Europe, while the German leader, Kaiser Wilhelm, hoped a war would distract attention from problems at home.

So, when Russia announced it was going to send troops to fight Austria, Kaiser Wilhelm quickly declared war on Russia. The next day, Adolf joined exuberant crowds on the streets of Munich, cheering and singing their national song, *Deutschland Uber Alles* (Germany over all the world).

Adolf was among the first men to volunteer for the German army. The fact that he was Austrian was overlooked and within a month he was recruited to one of the local battalions.

This enlargement shows Hitler celebrating the news of war in 1914.

By now, France and Britain had agreed to fight alongside Russia against Austria and Germany. As winter approached, Adolf was sent to a battlefield on the western front. His role was to take messages to and from the front line. It was a dangerous job that he did with pride. In December he was awarded a medal – the Iron Cross, Second Class. Nothing could have made him happier.

Adolf was a curiosity among his fellow soldiers. He received no mail from family or friends, never drank or smoked and didn't seem to believe in having fun. As the others chattered about things they missed, Adolf sat reading or painting.

"Have you never loved a girl?" asked one of the soldiers.

"I've never had time for anything like that," answered Adolf, sharply.

The only thing he cared for was a little dog he'd adopted – a white terrier who had strayed across enemy lines. Adolf named him Foxl and taught him tricks. "He obeys only me," noted Adolf, with satisfaction.

But when his battalion was ordered to move on, his dog was nowhere to be seen. Adolf was livid. "Someone must have stolen him," he thought. He never saw Foxl again.

Two years into the war, at the Battle of the Somme, a shell exploded in Adolf's dug-out and he was wounded in the thigh. He begged to stay, but was sent to a hospital in Germany. There, Adolf was appalled by the low morale among the wounded.

Hitler, far right, with two other soldiers in 1914. His beloved dog Foxl stands by his feet.

"I shot myself in the foot to escape the front line," said a patient, smugly.

"I've persuaded the doctor I'm too ill to return," bragged another.

Adolf silently cursed the cowards.

When the doctors discharged him, he made a trip into Munich. But he found the war deeply unpopular there too. People blamed it for the harsh conditions at home.

"Do they not realize what we're fighting for?" Adolf fumed to himself.

He decided that the Jews were taking the best local jobs, rather than fighting on the front line, and this made him even angrier.

By spring, Adolf was back with the troops and much happier. Never before had his days been so structured and rewarding. One morning, when the phone lines were down, he risked his life delivering a message. The army rewarded his bravery with the Iron Cross – First Class this time. Adolf swelled with pride.

But the fortunes of war were changing. A few months later, Adolf was in the messengers' dug-out when a shell exploded. The ground trembled, scattering clods of earth. His eyes began to sting. He blinked furiously, but the pain simply grew more intense. "Mustard gas!" he gasped.

Guided by another soldier, he stumbled out of the dug-out and away from the front line. For Adolf, the war was over.

German soldiers emerge from a cloud of poison gas. Hitler experienced a similar gas attack in 1918.

Government troops try to stamp out a revolution in Germany, 1919.

Chapter 4

Betrayal

Still recovering from temporary blindness, Adolf heard talk of defeat and a revolution in Germany. "Never!" he told himself. But a few days later his worst fears were confirmed.

"Our troops have surrendered," announced a solemn pastor to the hospital ward. "We are now at the mercy of our enemies."

For Adolf, the feeling of betrayal was unbearable. He had given five years of his life fighting for a greater Germany.

"And now all is lost," he muttered into his pillow. "It has all been in vain."

After years of bloody fighting, most Germans craved peace. But Adolf wanted revenge. He heard that Communists and Jews were behind the revolution. "So it's *their* fault that Germany has to sign a crippling peace treaty," he raged.

The Treaty of Versailles, imposed by Britain, France and America, forced Germany to give up land, reduce its army and pay huge sums of money for war damage. Very soon, Germans were suffering from high unemployment and rising prices.

After the war, most soldiers didn't have a job. Some ended up begging for money.

Like many soldiers, Adolf had no job to return to. Now aged 29, his only plan was to stay with the army for as long as possible. Once again, the future looked bleak. But then he met Captain Karl Mayr and everything changed.

"Our mission is to stamp out negative thoughts in the army," said the captain. "We want officers to attend our courses."

Adolf was one of the first officers to sign up. He attended lectures on politics, history and economics, and was fascinated by the content. One lecturer, Professor von Müller, claimed that the Jews were squeezing too much money from the German economy.

"But Jews are just good businessmen," said an officer as they were leaving.

Adolf turned on him instantly. "No they're not," he snapped. "They are the very source of Germany's misfortunes!"

Adolf proceeded to lecture those around him on why the Jews were a curse on society. His determined, guttural voice reached across the room.

"Who *is* that man?" the professor asked. "He's a natural speaker."

"It must be Adolf Hitler," replied Captain Mayr.

Within a month, the captain appointed Adolf to give his own lectures. It was a challenge that Adolf embraced with passion. He wanted his fellow officers to share his belief in Germany's greatness.

Hitler clenches his fists defiantly in one of his many speeches.

One day in September, Mayr sent Adolf to report on a meeting of a new political group – the German Workers' Party. After the guest speaker sat down, a heated debate broke out. Adolf couldn't resist taking part and his impassioned speech silenced the others.

"Goodness, he's got a mouth," whispered the party chairman. "We could use him."

A week later, Adolf was invited to join the German Workers' Party. It seemed a small, amateur group to him, but one where he could make a difference. He became party member 555 and was soon speaking at all their meetings.

Word got around about the talented new speaker and Adolf started attracting large crowds. He spoke simply, but with conviction. He knew what people wanted to hear and he repeated the same messages again and again.

"We were betrayed at the end of the

A painting from the 1920s shows Adolf Hitler speaking to party members at a small meeting.

war," he told his audience. "The Jews and Communists are to blame. We must unite against them and become a mighty nation once more."

These ideas weren't new. Many small parties were saying the same thing. But Adolf had an advantage – he knew how to make people listen. He waited out of sight until the meeting hall was packed. Then he marched into the crowd and climbed onto a table.

Eventually, when there was absolute silence, he began to speak. He talked of revenge, anger and hatred. And, as the cheers from the crowd grew louder, he repeated the party's slogan: "We will go our way unshakably to our goal."

Soon, Adolf was discharged from the army and got a full-time job working for the German Worker's Party. The words "national" and "socialist" were added to their name, and from their initials – NSDAP in German – came their nickname, the Nazi Party.

But Adolf didn't always agree with how the party was run. After one quarrel with the leaders, he stormed out. "I will only return if you make *me* the leader," he threatened. The Nazi Party relied heavily on their top speaker. They had no choice but to elect him.

Adolf returned to the party with increased enthusiasm. He introduced the Stormtroopers, a group of brown-shirted guards. Then he designed a striking banner for the party –

a black swastika in a white circle on a red background.

This is what Hitler's Nazi banner looked like. The swastika shape in the middle was originally a Hindu symbol for the sun.

Each week there were grand rallies and demonstrations to show off the Nazis' strength. They consisted of marching, music, singing and speeches. By giving the party a high profile, Adolf hoped more people would join. Another recruitment tactic was violence and fear.

"People need a good scare," Adolf told other Nazis. "Haven't you noticed, after a brawl at a meeting, the ones who get beaten up are the first to apply for membership?"

When a rival party leader was speaking in town, Adolf sent some Nazis to storm the stage. A big fight ensued, and Adolf ended up spending a month in prison. But this didn't stop him. In his mind, any publicity was good publicity.

Adolf's reputation was growing steadily. Several rich, influential men were impressed by his speeches and donated large sums of money to the Nazis. One donor, Ernst Hanfstaengl, invited Adolf to dinner. He was shocked that this eloquent speaker, with a deep appreciation of Wagner, could have such atrocious table manners. Adolf hardly knew how to hold a knife and fork, and he rudely added sugar to the very best wine.

With extra money from members' fees and meetings,

the Nazi Party was doing well. Meanwhile, Germany's economy was in big trouble. As the country struggled to meet its huge war repayments, its money system collapsed. Most people couldn't even afford a loaf of bread.

Adolf saw this situation as an excellent opportunity to gain power. He marched into a local government meeting and ordered his Stormtroopers to sieze the politicians. "The national revolution has begun!" Adolf proclaimed. His plan was to take over the whole country. Thinking the politicians were on his side, he let them go. But he was wrong. The next day, when 2,000 Stormtroopers entered Munich, the police and army were waiting. In the chaos that followed, 16 Nazis were killed and Adolf dislocated his shoulder. He was later arrested.

In this photograph, Hitler addresses some of the Nazis who helped him attempt a revolution in 1923.

Chapter 5

Mein Kampf

This time, Adolf was in prison for 13 months. Far from punishing him, the prison guards treated him with respect. They gave him a large, comfortably furnished room, where he regularly received mail, gifts and visitors. He spent hours reading works by great philosophers and soon decided to write his own book. As the days went by, he dictated pages of notes about his life and his view of the world.

In prison, Hitler was allowed to read newspapers and drink tea.

His words exposed his passionate hatred of Jews and Communists, and his belief that blonde, blue-eyed 'Aryans' were the world's superior race. "All those who are not racially pure," he wrote, "are simply waste."

He went on to describe his vision for the nation. "Germany will either be a world power," he claimed, "or there will be no Germany." His long-term ambition was to conquer more *Lebensraum* (living space) for the pure, Aryan Germans.

Shortly after Adolf's release from prison, his notes were published by the Nazis, under the title *Mein Kampf* (My Struggle). At first, there was little interest in the book, but it eventually sold millions of copies.

At the age of 35, Adolf resumed his role as leader of the Nazi Party with

An English edition of *Mein Kampf*, 1939

renewed energy. To come to power legally, he needed to win the hearts and minds of the people. This wasn't going to be easy. The German economy was recovering fast, thanks to large loans from the USA. Germans were enjoying their everyday lives and they weren't interested in a radical change.

So Adolf focused on building up the party structure instead. He also introduced the Hitler Youth Movement, to promote Nazi ideas through songs, sports and games.

Away from politics, Adolf continued to lead a simple life. He rented a cheap apartment and ate a basic vegetarian diet. Once he was asked to give a wedding speech, but he refused. "I must have a crowd when I speak," he explained. "In a small, intimate circle I never know what to say."

The person closest to him was his niece, Geli. He adored her and persuaded her to live with him. But Adolf became intensely jealous when she spent any time with other men. Before long, he refused even to let her out of the apartment without a chaperone.

"My uncle is a monster," Geli complained to a friend. "No one can imagine what he demands of me."

Then, one morning in September, 1931, Adolf received the devastating news that Geli was dead – shot by his own pistol. The Nazis declared the death an accident, but it was more likely that she had taken her own life. For a week, Adolf was inconsolable. For the rest of his life he kept a photo of Geli by his bedside.

Geli Raubal, Hitler's niece. This picture was taken by Hitler's photographer, Heinrich Hoffmann.

After Geli's funeral, Adolf became even colder and more calculating. He took a young lover, Eva Braun, but refused to be seen with her in public. Mostly, he plunged himself into politics... and found that events were finally swinging his way.

A sudden collapse of the US economy broke Germany's spell of prosperity. Businesses went bust overnight and the nation plunged into a depression. Adolf followed the news hungrily. The time was ripe to promote extreme Nazi politics.

In his speeches, he criticized the Treaty of Versailles and blamed the Jews and Communists for Germany's problems. Only the Nazi party, he argued, could lead the nation to a brighter future.

Desperate for a new government, Germany held a series of elections. Adolf campaigned harder than anyone. He impressed voters by arriving in a plane. This meant he could visit 21 cities in just one week. Meanwhile, his Stormtroopers paraded down the streets, Nazi films were shown in as many places as possible and posters of Hitler were plastered everywhere.

As a result, the Nazis gained an incredible 36% of the vote. They were still short of the majority they needed to rule, so Adolf demanded that the President, von Hindenburg, make him Chancellor (Prime Minister of Germany) instead. If not, he warned that the powerful Nazis would cause mayhem. After weeks of negotiating, von Hindenburg reluctantly gave in.

A poster (left) promotes Hitler as Germany's leader. A voting card (below) shows his name selected.

13·MÄRZ 1938
EIN VOLK EIN REICH
EIN FÜHRER

Reichstag für Freiheit und Frieden
Wahlkreis

Nationalsozialistische Deutsche Arbeiterpartei

Adolf Hitler

Heß   Frick   Göring   Goebbels

Within a month, the German parliament building had been set alight. The fire gave Adolf the perfect excuse to take action, especially since the chief suspect was a Communist.

"We must crush out this murderous pest with an iron fist," Adolf stormed.

First, he ordered the assassination of many Communists and other rival politicians. Then he introduced a new law – the Enabling Act – which gave him emergency powers for the next four years. In other words, he could do as he pleased without needing anyone else's approval. Many Germans were shocked, but others were pleased to see their new Chancellor act so decisively.

After a decade of struggle and persistence, Adolf Hitler's rise to power was complete.

Chapter 6

Road to war

In his election speeches, Hitler had spoken of peace and stability, but his real goal was world domination.

"The next five years have to be devoted to rendering the German people capable of bearing arms again," he told cabinet members in a secret meeting. The members were all hand-picked by Hitler. Goebbels was Head of Propaganda and Culture, Göring was Chief of the Secret Police and Himmler was in charge of an elite team of bodyguards – the SS.

Hitler looks out over a sea of troops at a Nazi rally in Dortmund, 1933.

In public, Hitler decided to clean up the Nazi's aggressive image. He was concerned that the Stormtroopers had too much power, so he plotted a ruthless act of treachery. During a bloody night of terror – the Night of the Long Knives – he sent Himmler's SS to round up over a hundred Stormtroopers and murder them.

Many Germans were relieved to be rid of these thugs. But Hitler had found a more cunning way to dominate. He set up a secret police force – the Gestapo – to spy on all Germans. Anybody speaking out against the Nazis risked imprisonment... or worse.

The people hardest hit by the Nazi leadership were the Jews. Hitler introduced new laws preventing them from being German citizens, holding important jobs or marrying pure, Aryan Germans. Then he banned all Jews from German schools and public places.

Hatred of the Jews was actively

encouraged. In just one night, Nazis burned down 200 Jewish synagogues, destroyed 7,500 Jewish shops and businesses, and murdered 91 Jews. Meanwhile, the SS arrested 26,000 more Jews and herded them into prisons known as concentration camps.

The plan was to make life for Jews so unbearable that they would leave the country. It worked. Within six years of Nazi rule, half the Jews in Germany had fled to other countries in search of a better life.

The Nazis persecuted Jews in other countries too. Here, a boy in Poland is forced to cut his father's beard, 1939.

Hitler's next plan was to conquer more living space for the German people. The Versailles Treaty forbade German troops from entering the Rhineland – a region along the border with France. Hitler decided to challenge this by marching soldiers into the area. There was no reaction from France or Britain. "So far, so good," thought Hitler.

Two years later, he sent troops into Austria. There was great excitement on the Austrian streets, but many people felt uneasy.

Hitler himself led a procession from Munich to Vienna. He stopped at Linz to put a wreath on his parents' grave and a crowd of locals gathered to greet him.

Nazi supporters welcome Hitler's troops to Austria in 1938.

"It was God's will," he declared, "to send a young man from here to rule Germany."

Hitler's next target was Czechoslovakia. His excuse was to liberate the border area named Sudetenland, where he claimed German citizens were being mistreated. The British Prime Minister, Neville Chamberlain, flew to Germany and tried to dissuade him, but the German leader was adamant. "I am prepared to risk a world war!" he cried.

Britain and France reluctantly agreed that Hitler could take over Sudetenland, so his troops met no resistance when they marched over the border. But they didn't stop there. Soon all of Czechoslovakia was under Nazi rule.

Hitler's pact with Stalin surprised many people. Here a cartoonist makes fun of their unlikely friendship.

Next, Hitler had his sights set on Poland, but he was wary of the Russians. Would they come to Poland's aid, as they'd done with Serbia? To be safe, he made a non-aggression pact with Russia's Communist leader, Joseph Stalin. It was a drastic move, since Hitler's and Stalin's politics were poles apart, but it was convenient for them both.

With the Russians on his side, Hitler fearlessly attacked Poland. To his surprise, Britain and France decided he'd gone too far. They swiftly declared war on Germany.

Chapter 7

The end

Hitler faced the prospect of war with frenzied excitement. He wore his army uniform with pride when addressing his people. "And I shall not take it off until after the victory... or I shall not live to see the end," he pronounced.

Britain and France could do nothing to help the Poles and within six weeks Poland was in German hands. Hitler paraded victoriously along the front line. He believed he was invincible.

Hitler studies a battle in progress in Poland, 1939.

Over his seven years in power, Hitler had built up a huge army and air force, with massive numbers of planes, tanks and trucks. Now he used them to great effect, conquering Denmark and Norway, and launching attacks on France.

By this time, French troops were stationed all along Germany's western border. But Hitler distracted them by invading the Netherlands and Belgium. As the French and British responded by moving north, German tanks broke through to the south and advanced into France.

A month later, a triumphant Hitler drove into Paris.

Hitler poses in front of the Eiffel Tower, 1940.

Only a narrow stretch of sea now lay between Hitler and the British Isles. He launched an aggressive bombing blitz on Britain, hoping the heavy casualties would force them to surrender. But the new British Prime Minister, Winston Churchill, was determined to fight to the end.

Hitler watched, frustrated, as the British air force won the battle of the skies. Eventually, he gave up and turned his attention east. Recklessly breaking his pact with Stalin, he now sent his troops into Russia.

The Russian troops were slow to respond, but mighty in number. By November, German forces were engaged in bitter warfare, as the temperature plummeted below freezing.

Hitler failed to conquer Russia before winter. His troops suffered in icy conditions.

Meanwhile, Japan was expanding its own empire. A vicious, surprise attack on the US naval base of Pearl Harbor forced America to retaliate. To show his approval of Japan's actions, Hitler rashly declared war on America. This left the Americans little option but to enter the war themselves. Suddenly, Hitler's enemies had a powerful new ally.

As for the people in Germany and other Nazi-occupied countries, they were powerless against the whims of their leader. Jews, disabled people, gypsies and protestors were herded into concentration camps and forced to work in appalling

Prisoners close to starvation in a Nazi concentration camp

conditions. Many starved to death, while others were killed by firing squads.

Hitler called for the extermination of Jews in order to 'cleanse' the human race. But the numbers involved were becoming unmanageable. He handed the problem over to the SS leaders, Heinrich Himmler and Reinhard Heydrich. Together they devised a horrific 'final solution' – the mass murder of Jews by poison gas.

While millions of innocent men, women and children were led to their deaths, the Nazis continued to wage war all over the world. But they were no longer winning.

News of defeat in Africa and Russia enraged Hitler. He retreated to his forest hideaway, known as the Wolf's Lair, where his health began to deteriorate. Pounding headaches and sleepless nights only made his temper worse. He preferred to spend the days making models for new German towns, with only his dog Blondi for company.

But these towns would never be built. British and American troops had landed on the French coast and were now marching on Germany. Meanwhile, victorious Russian troops were advancing from the east. Few Nazis dared tell Hitler the truth – they were too afraid of his temper.

The following month, a courageous German colonel attempted to blow up the Nazi leader. While others died, Hitler walked away with just a few cuts and bruises. "I am immortal!" he cried. But his joy was shortlived.

By now, Hitler's enemies had reached Germany. He returned to the capital city, Berlin, where continuous air raids forced him to take shelter in a vast bunker underground. A few faithful followers gathered around him, including his mistress, Eva.

Hitler began dictating his version of the war. He blamed defeat on everyone except himself and showed no pity for the German people. "Those who remain after the battle are inferior," he claimed, "for the good will have fallen."

The heartless leader took comfort in one vile, deluded thought. "We have lanced the Jewish abscess," he said, "and the world of the future will be eternally grateful to us."

As Berlin crumbled around him and other Nazis spoke of surrender, Hitler resolved to kill himself. But first he surprised everyone by marrying Eva. "She returned of her own free will to share my fate," he declared.

The following morning, Blondi was sent to be poisoned. Hitler closed the door on himself and his wife. He watched Eva swallow a poison capsule. Then he held a pistol to his head and pulled the trigger.

A bust of Hitler lies in the ruins of his Berlin headquarters, 1945.

Hitler's life

1889 – Adolf Hitler is born in Austria.

1903 – His father dies.

1905 – He leaves school and lazes around at home.

1907 – Hitler fails to get into art school. His mother dies
and he moves permanently to Vienna. Within a
few years, he is on the streets.

1913 – Hitler's inheritance comes through and he moves
to Munich.

1914 – The First World War begins. Eagerly, Hitler joins
the German army.

1918 – Hitler is temporarily blinded. He's recovering in a
hospital when he learns of Germany's defeat.

1919 – Hitler discovers his gift for public speaking.

1921 – The Nazi Party makes Hitler their president.

1923 – Hitler attempts a revolution and is imprisoned.
He starts work on *Mein Kampf*.

1925 – Hitler leads the Nazis once more. He forms his
own army, the Stormtroopers.

1929 – The German economy collapses.

1931 – Hitler's beloved niece, Geli, dies in his apartment.

1933 – Hitler is appointed Chancellor. He passes the
Enabling Act and takes control of Germany.

1936 – German troops enter the Rhineland.

1938 – Germany takes over Austria.

1939 – Germany invades Czechoslovakia, then Poland.
The Second World War begins.

1945 – Hitler marries Eva Braun and commits suicide.